# FREEDOM FROM TYRANNY

## H.J. Grahame

ISBN: 978-0-9942158-2-6

# Table of contents

# Emergency

I'm a good teacher, but even I have difficulty explaining how the money system works. In a nutshell, it's a complicated mess which benefits a few and undermines everyone else.

My own journey of learning began after a motorcycle accident. Both my legs had broken and I was bound to a wheelchair for several months. With time on my hands, I decided to research some topics that interested me, and one of those topics was taxation.

In particular, I disliked paying income tax. I thought it was unreasonable that the government – or anyone – could demand money from me. I also didn't like what the government spent my tax dollars on.

So I googled taxation. But all I found were reported incidences of other people trying to avoid paying tax and not succeeding. Inevitably, too, such people were ridiculed and attacked as fools or moral delinquents.

From there, I moved onto YouTube videos and, lo and behold, I came across a short video of an Australian man who honestly and candidly stated that he didn't pay income tax. I was intrigued. The story he gave as to how he became a non-taxpayer was even more intriguing.

Let's call him Tim. Tim described that, one day, he noticed that his name on tax documents was always written in capital letters. Tim found this curious and, in all innocence, telephoned the taxation department and asked why his name was spelt in capital letters.

The response was totally unexpected. The tax department said, "That's okay, you don't have to pay tax anymore". Tim said, "No, no. I'm happy to pay tax. I just want to know why my name is written in capital letters." Again, no explanation. Again, just the statement, "You don't have to pay tax".

From that moment, I was hooked. I became a super sleuth on a mission, searching for any clues as to what was really going on. My investigations led me to writers and speakers in the United States who talked about names in all-capital letters. They also spoke about the banking industry, governments and courts. I grabbed whatever information I could. And I'm glad I did, because some of the most useful websites would later mysteriously disappear.

I don't have all the pieces of the puzzle, but the pieces I do have make for a very interesting and informative story to tell.

# Strawman

There are two legal entities. There is the flesh and blood, breathing, living you and then there is a legal entity which has your name spelt in all-capital letters. Sometimes that all-capitals entity is referred to as the strawman.

If you look up the meaning of "strawman" in a dictionary, you'll find that it means a deliberately misleading proposition or a person who has no substance or integrity.

The strawman legal entity which has your name in all-capital letters was created by the government at around the time you were born. It has no flesh-and-blood substance, and it is deliberately misleading because, when someone sees their name written in all-capital letters, they assume it is referring to their self when, in fact, it is referring to a government-created strawman.

When you notice your own name written on a document in capital letters, know that that name is not referring to the real you. Instead, it is referring to the strawman, which is a non-living legal entity created by the government.

# Person

If I say the word "person", you probably conjure in your own mind an image of a flesh-and-blood human being. Back in Roman times, however, the word "person" meant "mask", and we see this association still today in the use of the word "persona".

The legal profession has its own unique definition of the word "person". Black's Law Dictionary (2$^{nd}$ edition, published in 1910), states that a person can be natural, artificial or juridical:

> *Natural person – A human being, naturally born, versus a legally generated juridical person.*
> *Artificial person – A nonhuman entity that is created by law and is legally different owning its own rights and duties.*
> *Juridical person – Entity, as a firm, that is not a single natural person, as a human being, authorized by law with duties and rights, recognised as a legal authority having a distinct identity, a legal personality. Also known as artificial person, juridical entity, juristic person, or legal person.*

In a later version of Black's Law Dictionary (7$^{th}$ edition, published in 1999), the distinction between a natural person and an artificial person is still made, however a corporation is also now considered to be a "person":

*Person:*   *1. A human being.*
*2. An entity (such as a corporation) that is recognized by law as having the rights and duties of a human being.*

Crazy stuff, hey.

# Corporation

For a long time, I believed that the strawman was a corporation created by the government. This was because many corporations have their titles in all-capital letters, just as the strawman does. And, also, a corporation is legally defined to be a "person".

Interestingly, corpses have their names in all-capital letters too. You'll notice this if you look at the tombstones in cemeteries.

The words "corpse" and "corporation" both derive from the Latin word "corpus" which means "body". Just as a corpse is a body without life, a corporation is a fictional body without real life. Living people can do valuable work, but a corporation cannot do work because it is a concept which has no real substance.

Whilst previously I believed that the strawman is a corporation, I've since learned that for a corporation to exist, it must be legally incorporated. And it's unlikely that governments worldwide go through the incorporation process for each and every strawman they create.

The strawman is therefore more accurately described as an artificial person.

# Deceit

To understand why the government creates these strawman entities, we need to go back in history.

The United States of America was colonised by European settlers in the 17<sup>th</sup> and 18<sup>th</sup> centuries. The expeditions were hugely expensive because they required the building of large sailing ships and also the provision of supplies for settlement in the new land. Money was borrowed from European banks and wealthy financiers, who charged interest on their loans. Thus, from the very beginning, the United States was a country in debt.

In time, a government sprang up which became responsible for the repayment of these colonisation debts. But the loans had become so large and accrued so much interest that it was impossible to pay them off. The United States government was stuck in a state of virtual bankruptcy.

The bankers, of course, wanted their money back. And, in 1933, a scheme was hatched whereby the government's loans and interest would effectively be paid back by the people. Each working person's income would be taxed and the tax dollars collected would be used to pay off the government's debts to foreign creditors.

But there was one very significant problem with the scheme. It is not right or lawful for a person (be they natural or artificial) to pass their debt onto another without the other's agreement and consent. Thus, the government could not lawfully pass its debts onto living people without their agreement.

And this is where the strawman illusion comes in.

The government creates a strawman entity utilising a living person's name. The government's strawman is an artificial person and has its title in all-capital letters.

The government issues a debt notice (such as an income tax notice) with the strawman name on it and posts it to the address of the living person. The living person is fooled into thinking that the debt notice is in their name and agrees to pay it.

# Fairness

This is why Tim from the YouTube video no longer needs to pay income tax. His curiosity unveiled the government's deceit. The tax department could not demand that Tim, the living being, pay the debts of the government or its strawman.

You, too, can pass any debt notice in the strawman name back to the issuer saying "This isn't me" or "This isn't my debt to pay". This includes not only income tax debts but also things like driving infringement notices, parking tickets, and even court fines that are in the all-capitals strawman name. Later in the book, I describe how you can do this in a more formal way.

Responding to a bill becomes somewhat more complicated, however, when the living you has received a benefit and the bill is in the name of the strawman. In that case, it is fair and reasonable that you pay for the benefit that you received.

A good example of this is when you receive credit from a bank via a credit card. The plastic credit card and the credit card account will both be in the name of the strawman, but, because you benefitted from the use of the credit, it is fair that you pay the debt which is in the strawman name. And, indeed, if the case were ever to go to court, the bank could say that you signed a contract whereby you willingly agreed to pay the amounts owing.

Some legal minds have said that because citizens receive benefits from the government (such as schools, hospitals, roads, pensions, police, etc) it is fair that they pay income tax. You may personally agree with this philosophy and decide to continue paying income tax, or maybe not. That is your decision to make.

For me, however, I prefer not to pay income tax. I don't want my money paying for weapons of war, subsidising pharmaceutical drugs or logging industries, or paying billions of dollars each year in interest on the government's loans. Most of all, I don't want to pay the wages of politicians who impose their laws upon me, telling me what I can and cannot do. I have a perfectly good moral conscience and I don't wish to be ruled over.

Rather than give a portion of my income to a bunch of bureaucrats who then spend it on my behalf, I would prefer to decide for myself which parts of the human community I give my money to.

# Taxation

There is a lot more to taxation than just personal income tax. The government often imposes several different taxes to ensure that it receives enough money to fund its operations and provide services and infrastructure to the community.

The figures vary from country to country, but about 30 to 60% of all tax revenue is from income tax. Income tax, however, includes not only tax paid by individuals but also the tax paid by companies and corporations. Some industries, such as banks and mining companies, pay billions of dollars in company income tax each year because their profits are so large.

Whilst there are a few exceptions to the rule, the governments of most countries receive far more in individual income taxes than they do from company income taxes.

In the United States, about 40% of all tax revenue is from social security contributions and Medicare tax. These are taxes that employers and employees must pay which fund the government's unemployment pensions, disability pensions, old-age pensions and healthcare programs – although, in reality, insufficient money is collected to fund the programs.

As well, there are taxes on property and sometimes taxes on the sale of goods and services.

Some governments also impose a payroll tax, which is paid by employers, and the amount of payroll tax increases with the number of people they employ.

# Bonds

Governments borrow money through the sale of government bonds. These are sometimes called government securities, treasury bonds, or just treasuries.

A bond is a promise to pay. When the government sells a bond, it receives a batch of money and promises to pay it back at a later time, when the bond matures. Different bonds mature at different times (eg. 5 years, 15 years) but the maturity period is set when the bond is first issued and sold.

Throughout the life of the bond, the government pays the bond-buyer amounts in interest, usually a couple of times each year. Hence a bond acts like a type of loan.

The government creates a bond and then sells it on a trading market. Anyone can buy government bonds, even individuals, and the purchaser of a bond can, if they wish, later place the bond back onto the trading market and sell it onto someone else.

Government bonds are purchased by a variety of different stakeholders. Sometimes bonds are purchased by investors within the same country and sometimes they are purchased by foreign investors. An investor might be, for example, a bank or an investment institution. Or they might be the member of a ridiculously rich family who have accounts in Hong Kong,

Luxembourg or the Cayman Islands.  Government departments which manage social security and retirement funds are also often buyers of government bonds.

The mix of investors varies from country to country and it varies over time, too, as the government continues to pay off old bonds and issue new ones.  The sale of government bonds is also affected by political events, because investors will generally only buy bonds when they are confident that the country's economy is stable and their money will be returned to them.

# Birth

When a government sells bonds, it does so on the basis that it believes it will collect enough money from citizens to pay back the bond amount at maturity, as well as any extra money needed to pay interest during the term of the bond.

So a government bond is really a bond on the people, since it is the living people who will be providing the money to pay back the principal and interest on the bond. Without your knowledge or consent, the government has placed you into a state of bondage and made you the security or guarantor for its loans.

This first occurs at around the time of your birth. When a new child is born, a state authority creates a birth certificate for the new living being and registers it. A record of this birth certificate and its serial number is passed to the federal government's department of commerce or treasury. At around the same time, the federal government creates the strawman entity with the same name as the newborn child but with the name in all-capital letters.

Birth certificates provide the federal government with proof that a living person exists – a living person who is expected to give money to the government throughout their working life.

For each birth certificate, the government is able to estimate how long the person will live for, how much they are likely to earn, and, most importantly, how much money the government is likely to receive from them via taxes and other debts in the strawman name.

The government then uses this information to calculate how much money it can reasonably loan via bonds and be assured that the people will later pay back.

# Names

Since your birth certificate identifies the real, living you, the name on it will never be spelled in all-capital letters because that's how the government's strawman or artificial person is spelt.

Instead, the names on birth certificates are either all in title case (eg. Amanda Dorothy Bennett) or, more commonly, the given names are in title case with the surname or family name in all-capitals (eg. Amanda Dorothy BENNETT).

The writing of names in capital letters was apparently first used by the Romans. Roman law decreed that as a person lost more and more of their rights and status, their name would be written with more capital letters. This tradition was called "capitis diminutio" and meant "a diminishing of status through the use of capitalization".

Where only the initial letters of a name are capitalized (that is, title case), this signifies a minor loss of status and rights.

If, instead, the given names are written in title case and the family name is in all-capitals, this represents a medium loss of status and rights. It is appropriate, then, that many birth certificates print the person's name in this way because birth certificates are used by the government to bind living people into paying government debts.

The lowest status is that of a person who has their full name in capital letters.  In Roman times, this represented complete bondage or slavery.

The strawman, which has its complete name in all-capitals, is a fictional creation of the government.  It is a dead trading entity which is completely under the control of living beings and has no rights of its own.

# Accounts

In order to open a bank account, you'll need to present the bank with your birth certificate. And, once the account has been created, you'll notice that the customer name will either be the full strawman name, such as AMANDA DOROTHY BENNETT, or a truncated version, such as A D BENNETT. The truncated version is a clever twist used by banks because it could represent either the strawman or the real you. But it's probably safe to assume that it represents the strawman.

Because the name on the account is the strawman name, the money that's in the account belongs to the strawman and not to you. And since the strawman is a creation of the government, that means that it's the government's money in the account and not yours. For this reason, governments are able to take money from bank accounts to pay a strawman debt – or at least they threaten to do so.

If all bank accounts are in the strawman name, does that mean it's the government's responsibility to pay outstanding debts on bank loan and credit card accounts? Well, no. As mentioned earlier, a court of law will say that you benefitted from the use of such money and therefore it is your responsibility to pay it back.

Another really important thing to understand about banks is that banks' bookkeeping records involve lists of credits and debits rather than amounts of cash.  Credit is money that the bank owes to someone and debit is money that someone owes to the bank.

The money in your everyday bank account is not cash, it is credit, and credit is an "I owe you".  So the money in the account is really money that the bank owns and owes to you, the customer.

Previously, you probably thought you had a bank account with your money in it.  However, the truth is that the account is in the name of the government's strawman and the money that's in the account belongs to the bank.

# Acceptance

If you decide that you do not want to pay a bill in the strawman name, you can return it to the sender with a note saying "this isn't me" or "no contract".  Alternatively, you can perform what's called an "acceptance for value" (abbreviated A4V).

To do an acceptance for value, you write the following on the debt notice, on an angle as shown, preferably in red ink, and replacing the words in green with your own information:

It's not imperative that you use red ink and write on an angle, but it indicates that you're a living person who has red blood and that you're not a dead or artificial person.

The exemption number you provide will either be the serial number on your birth certificate or, if you are a resident of the United States, you can use the social security number without dashes. If you live in the United States, you write that the A4V is to be deposited to the U.S. Treasury but, if you live in a different country, you put that country's treasury instead.

The STRAWMAN FULL NAME is your full name in capital letters, and this will be the same as the debtor's name on the bill. If the bill is in your real name – that is, any of the given names are in upper and lower case – then you cannot perform an acceptance for value on that bill.

Once you have written the A4V words on the bill, make a copy of it for your records and then post the original back to the issuer. Do not send it to the address given for payments. Post it to the sender's address listed on the envelope.

The rationale behind A4V and why it works is quite complex, but I will attempt to explain it in simple terms.

When a government department posts out a debt notice in the strawman name, it is, in effect, posting a debt notice to itself because the strawman is a creation of the government. The debt, therefore, isn't a bona fide debt. It doesn't make sense for the government to owe money to itself. So, when the government first issues a strawman debt, the debt isn't "real".

If the receiver of the debt notice posts it back to the issuer saying "this isn't me" or "no contract", then the pseudo-debt falls back into the nothingness from which it came.

But if a living person accepts the debt notice, hangs onto it, and takes responsibility for it, then it becomes real. And once a strawman debt notice becomes real, then someone has to cough up the money. Obviously, if you decide to pay the debt, then you're accepting the debt notice and making it real.

When you perform an acceptance for value, you are also accepting the bill for the value listed on the bill and thereby making the debt real. And, now that it's real, someone has to pay it. But with an A4V, you send it back to the issuer and direct that the government's strawman is to be charged with the debt. In other words, the government will have to pay its own debt.

The government can – if it so desires – pay the debt using some of the money it received when it sold a bond using the living you and your birth certificate as security. The government did, after all, make you the surety for its loans without your knowledge or consent. Because you are a surety for the government's loans, you are an "authorised representative" and have the authority to direct that the government use such bond money to pay the debts of the strawman.

If you perform an A4V on a strawman bill and post it back, inevitably the government department will reissue the bill. They're hoping, of course, that you will pay it. Each time they send you a bill, though, you can perform yet another acceptance for value on it and post it right back. You can perform as many A4Vs as you wish.

The government department may then send you a letter claiming that the bill has not been paid. This is technically correct because payment involves the use of earned money and only living people can work and earn money. In contrast, an acceptance for value is an "offset" where a bookkeeping debit is offset with an equivalent amount of bookkeeping credit. But you can write back to them saying that the bill is not in your name.

Sometimes there is a coupon at the base of the bill notice, such as with tax notices. This coupon section is actually a money order, and you fill it out as though you were writing a cheque, putting the amount in figures into the empty box provided on the coupon (as well as writing the A4V on the main section of the bill). My understanding is that, by filling out this coupon section, you are creating the money which pays the bill. Again, use red ink and replace the green text with your own information:

Money Order, today's date
Pay to: U.S. Treasury
Pay: Twenty-three thousand dollars and ten cents, $23,000.10
By: Your full name in upper/lower case, exemption number
Void where prohibited by law

Then turn the page over and, on the back of the money order, write the following:

I personally have performed A4Vs on a variety of debt notices in the strawman name in Australia.  When I performed an A4V on a taxation bill and filled out the coupon section as above, the taxation department issued an amount of credit to offset the debt and provided me with documentation showing the balancing of the account to zero.

With all other strawman debts that I have A4Ved, the government agency has not provided me with any documentation showing an offsetting of the debt.  Instead, it has generally sent letters to me requiring payment three times before finally giving up.

# Creditor

If you perform an acceptance for value on a strawman debt, the government agency which issued the debt may threaten you and say they have the right to take money from your bank account to pay the outstanding debt.

All bank accounts are in the name of the strawman, and, since the strawman is an entity of the government, the government concludes that the money in the strawman bank account is theirs. Such is their desperateness.

You can, however, take control of the strawman and, when you do, you take control of all bank accounts and other property held in the strawman name.

To take control, you create a security agreement between your living self and the strawman. A security agreement is a legal document which is entered into when one person (the creditor) lends money to another (the debtor). If the debtor is unable to repay their debt to the creditor, the debtor's property is sold and funds from the sale go to the creditor.

Where a creditor and debtor have both signed a security agreement, the creditor becomes what is called a "secured creditor" because they now have some security that their money will be returned to them.

In our case here, the strawman is the debtor because it is the one which all the government's debt notices are issued to. The living you is the creditor, and this is because your contribution and work is valuable and gives money its value. Nature provides food, air and water for free so there's no need to pay nature. The money we use in society is solely there to attribute value to the work of a living person.

An example of a security agreement is given at the end of this chapter. You can use this for yourself, replacing the words in green with your own information. The serial number is any number you give it, such as a combination of your initials and today's date. The date is the date you sign it. You sign with your usual signature as the secured party, and you handwrite the name of the strawman in all-capital letters.

For a security agreement to have legal power, it must be placed on a public noticeboard. Fortunately, there is an international commercial noticeboard located in Washington D.C. which can be used by anyone in the world, and in the next chapter I describe how to place your security agreement on that noticeboard.

Once you have completed the security agreement process and you are the secured creditor, you have the highest claim on anything and everything that the strawman owns or has an interest in, such as the money in strawman bank accounts.

# SECURITY AGREEMENT

Serial number: ADB022420

NON-NEGOTIABLE        Date: Today's date

All Property of AMANDA DOROTHY BENNETT (or any derivative thereof), Debtor, of 22 Yellow Road, Wizard City, KANSAS 67428, U.S.A. is hereby the property and security of the Secured Party, Amanda Dorothy Bennett care of 22 Yellow Road, Wizard City, Kansas [67428] U.S.A., and before any of the following property can be exchanged, sold, tendered or in any manner disposed of, the Secured Party must be compensated for the property.

This property now owned and hereafter acquired includes, but is not limited to, proceeds, products, accounts and fixtures held by AMANDA DOROTHY BENNETT. Any property not specifically listed, named or listed is included in the same.

The Debtor agrees to notify all employers and creditors of the same, as all Debtor's property is of this date property of the Secured Party.

This privately held security agreement is not dischargeable in bankruptcy court as the property of the Secured Party is exempt from levy.

AMANDA DOROTHY BENNETT          ABennett
_____          _____
Debtor                           Secured Party

# Noticeboard

The international noticeboard where you can place your security agreement is called the UCC file.  The noticeboard took its name from the UCC or Uniform Commercial Code, which is a set of regulations that pertain to commercial transactions, but the noticeboard itself is not the set of regulations.

Placing a document onto the UCC noticeboard involves filing what's called a financing statement.  Once you have filed a financing statement wherein you attach your security agreement, the security agreement becomes a legally-binding document.

Here is a step-by-step guide to placing your security agreement onto the UCC noticeboard:

To begin, go the website
https://fortress.wa.gov/dol/ucc/

If the webpage is not loading, go to
https://fortress.wa.gov and then do a search for the phrase "UCC file and search online".  Clicking on the link will then take you to the correct page.

Click on "File a Financing Statement".

Here you enter the contact name and details for the document you are filing. These details will be displayed publicly, so avoid providing too much personal information. You certainly do not need to fill out every box in this section. Basically, just provide your name and a way of contacting you should someone want to ask you a question about your financing statement.

**Debtors**. The debtor is the strawman. The strawman is an organization, not an individual.
The surname is the strawman's surname written in all-capital letters. The first and any middle names are also written in all-capital letters. The city is the city in which the strawman is known to reside (that is, where any strawman bills get posted to). Select the state and country. All other fields here are optional. If you enter an address, put the address that strawman bills currently get posted to.

**Secured Parties**. There is only one secured party and it's you, the real person. You're an individual, not an organization. You write your surname with first letter capital, other letters lowercase. Same with the first and any middle names. The city is where the real you lives, along with the state and country. All other fields are optional.

If you provide an address, either provide a post office box or place "care of" in front of the address, and put the zipcode in square brackets. Technically speaking, your residential address is the address of the strawman whereas the "address" of the living you is your physical body. By putting "care of" in front of the residential address and putting square brackets around the zipcode, you're making it clear you're not the strawman.

**Collateral**. The collateral which is being filed is the security agreement which you have created and signed. You will need to turn your signed security agreement into a PDF file and upload the PDF file onto the UCC website. Then in the collateral box write the following (replacing the words in green with your own):

Document: Security Agreement, serial number ADB022420, dated February 24, 2020 (see attached)

**Additional Details**. Select the option "Collateral is held in a Trust". Select the option "Filing Type: A Debtor is a Transmitting Utility" (this causes the filing to last indefinitely; if you don't select transmitting utility then the filing only lasts for five years).

**Miscellaneous**. Select "None" for each of these options.

You are then taken to a page which shows how much it will cost to file the UCC financing statement (about $20) and fields for you to enter credit card information. This can be a credit card in someone else's name.

You are then shown a receipt for the transaction and you can print a copy of the receipt.

Click on "View Filing" next to the PDF logo. Then download the file onto your computer, and print a copy for your own records.

# Assignment

Whilst you can perform acceptance for values on all tax notices in the strawman name for the rest of your life, you can, instead, withdraw yourself from the income tax system altogether.

To withdraw from the system, you do what's called an "assignment of reversionary interest" of the birth certificate. Since the birth certificate is what the government uses as security when borrowing money, it represents the bond that has been placed upon you. When you assign the birth certificate to the government, you're passing the bond back to the government and essentially saying "I do not agree to be the surety for the government's debts".

The term "reversionary interest" is used in trusts and trust law. A trust is an arrangement where there is a grantor/trustor/settlor (person giving something), a beneficiary (person receiving something), and a trustee (person who ensures that the transfer occurs). Posting a parcel is a trust situation where the person posting the parcel is the grantor, the person receiving the parcel is the beneficiary, and the postmaster or mailman is the trustee.

If a beneficiary doesn't want to receive some part of a trust, they can assign it back to the grantor, which is called an "assignment of reversionary interest". It's a bit like posting a parcel back to the sender. Here, we're sending the birth certificate (and hence the bond on us) back to the government.

The assignment of reversionary interest can be performed on the UCC noticeboard website. First you file a financing statement in which you list the birth certificate as an item of collateral, and then you file what's called an amendment. On that amendment, you perform the assignment and assign the birth certificate to the government's Department of Treasury.

Before embarking on the assignment, you will need to obtain a recent copy of your birth certificate. Older versions may no longer be recognised legally, so it's best to purchase a new one. If you were born in the United States, you can purchase a birth certificate from VitalChek.

Next, you perform an acceptance for value on the birth certificate and assign it to the Treasury by writing the following words in red on the front and back of the certificate (replacing the words in green with your own information).

Front:

Accepted for Value, Assign for settlement and closure
Exempt from levy, Exemption ID# exemption number
Your signature, without recourse
Today's date
Deposit to the U.S. Treasury and charge the same to
STRAWMAN FULL NAME exemption number

Back (written parallel to the long edge
of the page):

Assign to U.S. Department of the Treasury
for deposit to U.S. Treasury
for account STRAWMAN FULL NAME exemption number
Your signature, without recourse

We are depositing the birth certificate to the Treasury (the
storehouse of government money) and assigning the birth
certificate to the Department of Treasury (the bureaucrats).

Here is a step-by-step guide to filing the financing statement and
amendment:

Go to https://fortress.wa.gov/dol/ucc/

File a new UCC financing statement where you are the secured party and the strawman is the debtor (as described in the previous chapter).  Remember to select "debtor is a transmitting utility".

Do not attach a PDF copy of your birth certificate as it can be used in identity theft.  Instead, just refer to it by putting the following description in the collateral box (replacing words in green with your own information):

Birth certificate for AMANDA DOROTHY BENNETT, registration number serial number on certificate, accepted for value and assigned in full to U.S. Department of the Treasury

After paying for this new UCC financing statement, keep a copy of it and note the file number it has been given.

Go back to https://fortress.wa.gov/dol/ucc/ and select "File an Amendment".

Enter your name and a method of contacting you should someone have a query with the filing, but do not provide too much personal information.  Select the state and country.  Enter the file number for the UCC filing you just did for the birth certificate.

**Amendment Details**. Select "Assignment".
In the first section you are giving the name of the person or entity you are assigning the collateral to, which in this case is the Department of Treasury. So select "organization" and for the organization name put "U.S. DEPARTMENT OF TREASURY", replacing the green initials with whatever country you are a citizen of.

Next, do an internet search and find the mailing address for the Department of Treasury in your country, and put that information in the relevant fields.

**Collateral**. As mentioned earlier, do not attach a PDF copy of your birth certificate. Instead, put the following in the collateral description:

> This is a full assignment of the following document: Birth certificate, registration number serial number on certificate

**Authorizing Party**. The real you is the secured party of record. So select "Individual" and enter your surname, first and any middle names with first letter capital and other letters lowercase.

File the amendment, pay for it, and keep a copy for your records.

Then either scan or take a photo of the A4Ved birth certificate (front and back) so that you can print copies of this in the future if you need to.

Once you've completed the assignment process on the UCC website, you then need to inform the government of what you've done and post to them a copy of all your documents, including the security agreement, A4Ved birth certificate, and all UCC financing statements and amendments. You might also want to include a cover letter, such as the one provided at the end of this chapter.

First, you'll be posting the original birth certificate that you A4Ved and copies of your other documents to the Secretary of the Treasury in your country. You can find the name and postal address of the Secretary on the internet.

Next, post a copy of all your documents to the taxation department and inform them that you are not a taxpayer. Having informed the taxation department of your assignment, they will no longer expect you to fill out taxation forms or pay income tax, and they will not come chasing you for money.

The only exception to this is if you have received a tax debt notice prior to performing the assignment. In that case, you will need to deal with that outstanding debt by performing an acceptance for value on it. If you have a tax lien (as occurs in the United States), then you will need to deal with that also before performing the assignment of the birth certificate. I describe in the next chapter how you can remove a lien.

Note, too, that assigning the birth certificate back to the government does not remove any liability you may have to pay company tax. Again, I tackle the topic of company tax in another chapter.

Lastly, neither the Department of Treasury nor the taxation department will formally acknowledge receipt of your documents, so it's best to post them by certified mail so you have proof that they were received.

Today's date
c/o 22 Yellow Road
Wizard City
Kansas [67428]

Dear sir/madam,

ASSIGNMENT OF REVERSIONARY INTEREST OF
BIRTH CERTIFICATE BOND IN THE NAME OF
AMANDA DOROTHY BENNETT
TO THE U.S. DEPARTMENT OF TREASURY

This letter is to inform you that I am no longer liable for debts of the corporate entity AMANDA DOROTHY BENNETT. That liability has been assigned to the Department of Treasury, as evidenced by the legal documents attached.

This assignment includes, but is not limited to, the payment of income taxes.

Yours sincerely,

ABennett

Amanda Bennett

# Liens

A lien is a way of seizing or gaining control of an asset of another person who owes money and is not paying their debts. It is a temporary transfer of the legal title of the asset to the creditor, and it prevents the borrower or debtor from doing anything with the asset.

The Internal Revenue Service in the United States (which, by the way, is not part of the U.S. government) places liens on individuals who have an outstanding tax debt.

In order for a lien to be effected, the debtor must be given several notices that the debt is due and payable. If there is no response from the debtor and the debt remains unpaid, then the lien is created. Some banking and government agencies also place liens on individuals for unpaid debts, but a lien can actually be imposed by any person who understands the process of how to create and enforce a lien.

Basically, liens seize your property. An IRS lien gives the IRS the right to take control of your assets (such as your home) in order to recoup money for a tax debt. If the lien is against your company, then the IRS can seize any money coming into the business. Whilst there is a lien on your home, you will not be able to buy or sell real estate, and getting a loan is extremely difficult.

To find out if you have any IRS liens, you can call the IRS Centralized Lien Unit on (800) 913-6050.

An IRS or government lien is addressed to the strawman in all-capital letters, so the lien is on the strawman and not on the real you.  It is the strawman which owes money to the IRS.  But if you are the secured creditor (because you have completed a security agreement and attached it to a UCC financing statement), then you are in control of the strawman.

Just as you can assign the birth certificate back to the Department of Treasury, you can assign a lien debt notice back to the IRS (or whoever issued the lien), thereby nullifying it.  This time, the lien notice is the item of collateral you list in the financing statement.

Note that there may have been new tax liabilities charged or paid since the lien was created, as well as interest or other penalties.  When you assign the lien, you are removing the lien but not these other outstanding tax debts, so you will have to deal with those separately using acceptance for value.

Here is a step-by-step guide to assigning a lien:

Get a copy of the Notice of Tax Lien from the IRS or whoever has placed the lien on the strawman.  Scan this document and create a PDF version of it.

Next, file a new UCC financing statement where the real you is the secured party and the strawman is the debtor.

Remember to select "debtor is a transmitting utility".
Attach the PDF of the lien notice document.
In the collateral box, describe the lien notice. For
example:

> Notice of Federal Tax Lien, **serial number** 320783305,
> **name of taxpayer:** AMANDA BENNETT, **prepared at**
> Kansas City, MO **on** 4 October 2022

After paying for this new UCC filing, keep a copy of it and
note the file number it has been given.

Go back to https://fortress.wa.gov/dol/ucc/ and select
"File an Amendment". Enter the file number for the UCC
filing you just did where the lien notice was the item of
collateral.

**Amendment Details**. Select "Assignment".
In the first section, you are giving the name of the entity
you are assigning the lien money to. Select
"organization" and enter the name and mailing address
of the agency or corporation that has issued the lien. For
example:

Internal Revenue Service, 324 25th St, Ogden, UT
84401, USA

**Collateral**. Attach your PDF of the notice of lien. In the collateral description box, enter the following information, replacing the words in green with your own information:

> This is a full assignment of the following document: Notice of Federal Tax Lien, serial number 320783305, name of taxpayer: AMANDA BENNETT, prepared at Kansas City, MO on 4 October 2015

**Authorizing Party**. Select "Individual" and enter your surname, first and any middle names with first letter capital and other letters lowercase.

File the amendment, pay for it, and keep a copy of it for your own records.

You will now need to inform the IRS (or relevant agency) as to what you have done. Post to them a copy of all your documents including the security agreement between yourself and the strawman, the UCC documents where you filed your security agreement, the lien notice, and your UCC financing statement and amendment where you assigned the lien. It is also worthwhile including a cover letter, and an example is given on the next page.

Today's date
c/o 22 Yellow Road
Wizard City
Kansas [67428]

Dear sir/madam,

## ASSIGNMENT OF LIEN

Please find enclosed a copy of a security agreement between myself, Amanda Dorothy Bennett, and the corporate entity debtor, AMANDA DOROTHY BENNETT, which was attached to a UCC financing statement on date of UCC filing.

Also enclosed is a copy of UCC documents filed on date of UCC filing evidencing an assignment of Notice of Federal Tax Lien, serial number 12345, in the name of AMANDA BENNETT, where the assignee is the Internal Revenue Service.

This is a full assignment of the lien, therefore the lien has been released.

Yours sincerely,

ABennett

Amanda Bennett

# Foreigners

If you were born in one country and now reside in another country, you may wonder if you can use the administrative processes I've described, such as acceptance for value, a security agreement, and assignments.

If you've ever received a document with your full name in capital letters from the government of the country you currently reside in, that means that the government has created a strawman and you can perform any of the above procedures on strawman debts.

The only difference is that, when performing an assignment of reversionary interest, you use the citizenship or naturalisation documents given to you by your new country rather than the birth certificate created by your birth country.

Your naturalisation documents will also have a serial number on them – just as a birth certificate does – and you use this as your exemption number when performing acceptance for values on strawman debts.

# Marriage

When you get married and change your name (or you legally change your name for any other reason), your new name is not automatically updated throughout the whole system. You will need to separately inform the tax department, banks, and the driving licence authority of any change to your name. When you do, the agency changes the name of the strawman on their accounts and files.

But you might be wondering: what name do I put as the secured creditor in my security agreement and UCC filings? Do I use my married name or the name given on my birth certificate?

You could probably use either, but personally I would use my current name and current signature, whatever that is. Similarly, if you've immigrated to a new country, I would use the name listed on the naturalisation certificate rather than any different name listed on the birth certificate.

# Registration

The word "registration" derives from the Latin prefix "reg" which means to rule, direct or control. It is closely associated with the word "rex" which translates as king or ruler. We see the prefix "reg" used in other words such as "regulations", "regime" and "regal".

As the word suggests, the act of registration enables some sort of rulership or control over the thing that is registered. In real terms, when an item is registered, the registration authority (be it a king, queen, or government) takes control of the legal title of the item.

There are two types of title: legal title and equitable title. Legal title is based on an official document which describes what an item is. Equitable title is who possesses an item because they paid for it. Technically, to fully own an item, you must have both legal and equitable title.

You might have purchased a piece of land and therefore have equitable title, however, if the title document for the land has been registered, then the registration authority (that is, the government) has control of the legal title.

A birth certificate is the legal title for a living being and so, when it is registered, the government takes control of the legal title of the human being. This apparently gives the government and its agencies, such as police, the right to assault and apprehend those who are not abiding by the government's rules and regulations.

The registration of birth certificates also supposedly gives the government the legal right to force medical treatments (such as vaccinations) upon children and to remove children from their families.

You can take back control of the legal title of a person – either your own or your child's – by placing the birth certificate as an item of collateral on a UCC financing statement where you are the creditor and the strawman is the debtor.  Once you have done so, you have the highest claim to the legal title of the living being, even if the legal title has previously been registered.

Some people do not want a birth certificate created for their child. They don't like the idea that their baby is being listed as an item of property belonging to the government.  They want their child to be free of government control.

If no birth certificate is created, then no strawman is created, and the child will never be expected to pay income tax or any other government debts.  However, without a birth certificate, a person is unable to get a bank account or passport and would not be able to access government services, Medicare or pensions, making their life much more difficult.

By having a birth certificate issued and then taking control of it by placing it on a UCC financing statement, you get the best of both worlds.

# Vehicles

Vehicles also get registered and, when they are, the government takes control of the legal title to the vehicle. That's why the police, marshals and sheriffs can take your car from you, even though you paid for it and have equitable title.

You might think, well, I'll just put the legal title of the car on to a UCC financing statement and then I will have full ownership of the vehicle. But it's not that simple.

Whilst a birth certificate is the legal title document for a living person and you can easily attach (or refer to) a birth certificate on a UCC financing statement, the legal title document for a vehicle is its manufacturer's statement of origin (MSO) and, unless you have the original MSO for the vehicle, you've got nothing to attach to a UCC filing.

When a new car is manufactured, the manufacturer issues the MSO which has on it a description of the car such as its make, model, engine number, and year of manufacture. Unfortunately, when someone buys a new car, the car salesperson automatically gives the MSO to the government.

To obtain an MSO for yourself, you will need to purchase a brand-new car and say to the car salesperson that you will only buy the car if you get to keep the MSO. This arrangement will only be possible if you fully pay for the car without any finance or loan agreements in place.

If you do ever purchase a new car and obtain the MSO for it, scan a copy of the MSO for your records and keep the original in your car.  Then, if you're ever stopped by a police officer, you can show them the MSO and they will have no right to touch, move or take your vehicle.

# Houses

In some parts of the world, land titles are registered too. The legal title document will have a description of the property and where it's located.

If you have purchased a piece of land, your name will be on the title document – or, rather, the strawman name will be on the title document. Here we go again!

Creating a security agreement between yourself and the strawman and placing that security agreement on the UCC noticeboard will give you control of the strawman and all property held in the strawman name. And you might think that that includes any real estate where the strawman is listed as the owner.

But here's the thing. The strawman is listed on the land title document as the registered proprietor, not the owner, and a registered proprietor is basically a tenant with private use of the land.

So even though you paid for the property with your hard-earned cash and therefore have equitable title, you do not own it fully because: (1) the property's legal title is registered and hence under the control of the government; (2) the legal title is in the name of the government's strawman; and (3) the strawman is merely a tenant and not an owner.

Because the government has control of the legal title to the property, it has the right to force you off the land or to compulsorily acquire it from you.

Even if you have entered into a security agreement between your real self and the strawman and you have also separately placed a copy of the land title document as an item of collateral on a UCC financing statement, you may need to convince a court or government agency that you now have control of the legal title to the property.

At the very least, because you are the secured creditor of the strawman, if the property were to be sold, you would have the first and highest claim to any proceeds from its sale.

# Company

Companies pay income tax, and, although the assignment of reversionary interest process removes any liability on you as an individual to pay income tax, the government will still expect your company to pay tax.

As with everything else that has significant monetary value, the government wants you to register your company so that it then has control of the legal title.

To keep control of the legal title, you might decide not to register your company with the government. This has the downside that you will not be able to open a business bank account, which you may need in order to access online trading and EFTPOs machines.

The other alternative is to register your company but place the registration certificate as an item of collateral on a UCC financing statement and, in the description section, provide any serial numbers or tax numbers associated with the company. You will also need to be the secured creditor, having previously entered into a security agreement with the strawman and placed the security agreement on a UCC financing statement.

Once you are the secured creditor of the strawman and you have taken control of the legal title of the company, you have the highest claim on any profits of the company. The government or any other agency (such as the IRS) therefore does not have the right to confiscate money or assets of the business in order to pay company tax debts.

I must point out, though, that I personally have never had a company and so I have not tested these particular ideas myself.

If I did have a company, I would go through the usual government processes in setting it up, and then I would pay myself a wage that is high enough to keep company profits – and therefore company taxes – to a minimum.

# Contractor

If you work for yourself or run your own business, you can do an assignment of reversionary interest and thus have no liability to pay individual income tax. However, if you're an employee of a company, it's a lot more difficult to avoid paying tax because employers are required to take out a portion of your wages and give it to the government.

I was employed in a new job recently, so I decided to experiment just to see what would happen. I was initially employed by a recruitment agency and placed on their payroll system. Then, after working on the job for about a month, I came off the agency's payroll system and was paid directly by the business I had been doing the work for.

When I was first employed by the recruitment agency, I was eager to present well and so I dutifully provided a taxation identification number (called a social security number in the United States). Regular tax instalments were thus taken from my salary.

After a few weeks, I was feeling more confident and secure in the job, so I wrote an email to the recruitment agency explaining that I don't pay income tax and therefore amounts for tax should not be removed from my wage.

The recruitment agency wrote back, asking if I had a document from the taxation department confirming that I do not pay tax. Although I had performed an assignment of reversionary interest and the taxation department no longer requested money from me, I had not been given any formal document stating that I was not a taxpayer. I suppose I could have attempted to explain to the recruitment agency that the strawman is the taxpayer, not the real me, but that would have required a long explanation that probably wouldn't get me very far.

So, I said to the recruitment agency that I wanted to withdraw the taxation identification number I had previously provided to them. The recruitment agency removed the number from their files, and I was immediately taxed at the highest rate possible, which meant that I lost about a third of my wage. I continued on this system until it came time to switch over to being employed by the company where I had been doing the work.

Having learned my lesson with the recruitment agency, I knew that it was pointless to explain to this next company why I don't pay income tax. So, instead, I said that I wanted to work for myself as an independent contractor and I would issue invoices to the company for the work I had performed. They agreed to the arrangement and we signed a contract.

As a self-employed independent contractor, I was not an employee of the company. I was therefore not on the payroll of the company, and the company had no duty to remove tax instalments from my wage. I did not receive other benefits from the company (such as sick leave, holiday pay, or health benefits) that I might otherwise have received if I were an employee, but I was okay with the arrangement.

I didn't pay any income tax on my earnings, which was the outcome I wanted.

# Pensions

Many people wonder: if I use acceptance for value or do an assignment of reversionary interest on the birth certificate, can I still apply for and receive government benefits such as Medicare and pensions? The answer is an absolute yes. I have done it myself.

The government's benefits are actually given to the strawman, not to the real you. If you ever receive money from the government, you'll notice that it is given to the all-capitals name and placed into a bank account which has the all-capitals name too. Medicare benefits will also be in the strawman name.

If you have entered into a security agreement with the strawman and placed it on a UCC financing statement, then you have the highest claim on any money held by the strawman, including such benefits. You can provide a copy of your UCC documents to the government department you're dealing with, but it's really not necessary and it tends to confuse the staff because they don't understand what they mean.

For philosophical reasons, you may feel uncomfortable receiving benefits from the government whilst not paying income tax, but that's a decision you'll have to make for yourself.

# Court

Courts are strange places. On the one hand, judges are meant to act as impartial observers and deciders of what is fair. But, on the other hand, they must first and foremost follow the laws and rules of the government.

This particular combination means that, for the most part, courts are there to do the bidding of the government. And, since governments want to get as much money as they can out of people via the strawman debtor entity, the courts play an important role in pressuring people to hand over money and give it to the government.

If, for example, you attempt to dispute an income tax debt in court, you will inevitably get smashed. If you dispute a driving charge or some other offence where the strawman is listed as the alleged offender, the court will use any and every form of manipulation to get the real you to agree to be the surety and payer of the debt.

During an arraignment where an accused offender is brought before the court, the judge describes the offence and then says to the accused person, "Do you understand the charge?" This is legal speak for "Do you stand under the charge?" and has nothing to do with whether you comprehend the charge or not. If you stand under the charge, then you are agreeing to stand under the rules of the court and be the payer of any strawman debt.

A charge is a debt. Just as you might charge up your phone with electricity, the government charges up or creates debts in the strawman name. The government hopes or expects real people to discharge these strawman charges and debts using either earned money or jail time as the method of payment.

If you want to pay the debts and charges of the strawman, go right ahead. You may feel guilty at having committed an offence and want to make reparations for your mistake.

However, if you have not hurt anyone and it's a case of the government screwing you for money, then you can refuse to pay the debts of the strawman and even refuse to participate in the court's processes. Also, you can perform an acceptance for value on any court document where the strawman is the debtor and hand it back to the judge or person who issued it to you.

If a litigant says to the judge that they are not the strawman all-capitals name, then often the case will just be thrown out. No court wants to publicly acknowledge the existence of the strawman or set a precedent which other people can follow.

Judges and lawyers are strictly bound by many rules and regulations. Even if their human side has empathy for a litigant, they cannot extend care because the laws prevent them from doing so. Courts are also under intense pressure to clear a backlog of cases waiting to be heard, and this has the unfortunate side effect of judges hastily jumping to conclusions.

If you have a dispute with someone – especially if it involves personal relationships or children – I strongly recommend that you find a mediator or counsellor who can help you achieve even a partial resolution outside of a court context, because arguing in court just leads to more hurt and more arguing.  Lawyers inevitably stir up arguments because it means they get paid more.

In an ideal world, judges would be mediators who assist people in resolving their disputes.  But, at the moment at least, the task of a judge is to attribute blame and impose punishment according to the rules and laws of the government.

# Banks

Central banks (sometimes called reserve banks) are completely different to the commercial banks that people interact with on an everyday basis.

Each country has a central bank, and it's responsible for ensuring that the country's currency remains relatively stable and the economy doesn't undergo a financial crisis. That's the theory anyway.

When central banks first came into existence, they were owned by wealthy banking families. For example, Nathan Rothschild was a key figure in the development of the Bank of England during the early 1800s. Nathan was one of five sons who had been sent by their father, Amschel Rothschild, to establish central banks throughout Europe.

Back in those days, central banks were a place where monarchies and governments could borrow large sums of money. In return for providing these large loans, a central bank gained the right to create and issue the country's currency.

One wonders how such private banks managed to amass more wealth than a monarchy in the first place, but it seems this was most probably the result of the monarchy spending all its money on wars in combination with some dodgy tax collectors who pocketed the taxes for themselves.

Today, most central banks are government-owned. The notable exceptions to this are the Federal Reserve of the United States and the central banks of Italy and South Africa, which are still completely in the hands of wealthy and powerful individuals. In some other countries, such as Japan, Greece, Turkey, Belgium and Switzerland, the central bank is owned by a mixture of government and private shareholders.

# Currency

Once upon a time, central banks printed new money as it was needed.  But those times have changed.

For many decades now, new money has been created by local commercial banks, and they create this new money whenever a customer takes out a loan.  The money that the bank gives to the customer is newly-created.

This newly-created money does not exist indefinitely, however.  As the customer makes principal repayments, the bank removes the repaid amount from the circulating pool of money and effectively destroys it.

With money being continually created and destroyed in this way, it's logical to expect the overall amount of money in the economy to be fairly stable.  But that's not what occurs.  The amount of money in existence is, in fact, growing exponentially, and the reason for this exponential growth is the interest charged on loans.

# Interest

Interest causes immeasurable harm to the economy and society.

Historically, most religions have deemed the charging of interest to be immoral. In the Middle Ages, the Catholic Church made it unlawful to charge interest on loans, and so in Europe at that time it was considered a crime. Back then, charging interest was called "usury", but nowadays "usury" generally refers to charging interest at especially high rates.

So what's so bad about interest? Well, I'll begin with the short version.

Rich people have money and poor people don't. The poor people require money to buy the items they need, but, if they don't have enough money, they must borrow it from the rich people. The rich people loan out their money to the poor people and charge an interest fee. That means that the rich get paid interest money despite doing no work and making no meaningful contribution to society. They just get richer and richer. And the poor get poorer because they always have to pay back more money than they receive.

The poor not only have to pay back more, but the money needed to pay the interest does not exist in the economy at the time it has to be paid. This creates a no-win situation for the borrower.

The only way the borrower can obtain the money to pay interest is by taking it from others in society (to their detriment) or by entering into another bank debt so that a new batch of money is created.

That debt has its own interest charges, and thus we have an ever-expanding economy where people are continually having to borrow more so as to create the new money which is needed to pay off yesterday's interest charges. It's like a whirlpool of debt that just gets larger and larger.

Interest also causes inflation or a rise in the price of all goods and services. When a business person (let's called them Person A) borrows money from a bank for their business, they attempt to pay the interest fees by raising the cost of the goods or services that they sell. If other people in the community then want to buy Person A's goods or services, they must also raise their prices so that they have enough money to purchase what they need. The effect ripples throughout society and ultimately all goods and services rise in price. Researchers have calculated that, on average, about 40% of an item's price is to cover interest payments of some type.

As well as raising the cost of goods and services, businesses try to avoid sinking into debt by keeping wages at a minimum and by pressuring employees to be more productive. Businesses also use manipulative advertising techniques in order to sell more of their goods and services, pushing them onto customers regardless of whether or not they're genuinely needed. Interest therefore causes consumerism.

Not everyone has their own business and can raise their prices, though. Employees are stuck with whatever salary they receive. And, if that salary is not enough to buy the items they need to live, then they must borrow money. Most people, for example, must take out a bank loan in order to buy a house. Some, too, use credit cards to pay for necessary items.

The only winners in this cruel game are those at the top of the financial heap who have no debts and "earn an income" by loaning money to others and charging interest on those loans. Everyone else is sinking deeper and deeper into debt and scrambling to stay afloat financially.

In an economy where new money is created via the loan process and where interest is charged on those loans, it is a mathematical certainty that indebtedness increases exponentially and that the system undergoes repeated collapses or recessions.

# Killing

The television and media channels will tell you that religious terrorists are killing people.  But television is a propaganda machine, designed to manipulate the thoughts of the masses.  It is not a source of absolute truth.  What students learn at school is also heavily influenced by those with wealth and power.

The reality is that bankers get rich from loaning money at interest.  And global financiers get extremely rich from loaning money to governments because the amounts involved are so large.

During times of war, governments have had to borrow a lot of money because they needed it to pay for weapons and the military, as well as to rebuild smashed cities and infrastructure.

Like a predatory wolf, global financiers have deliberately used propaganda and lies to stir up conflict and wars between people, and then loaned money to both sides of the war at interest.  It involves "making a killing" in more ways than one.

And, when war between countries isn't possible, the wolves use their wealth to bribe young, desperate people to commit acts of violence, rioting, and looting.

Religion, however, has been an ongoing thorn in the side of the financial elites.

Jews, for example, are not allowed to charge interest on loans to other Jews, and this has meant that members of the Jewish community help each other and have no need to go to a bank to borrow money. Their community thrives economically because the corrupting and destructive influence of interest is absent.

During World War II, some six million Jews were killed. It was a deliberate attempt at genocide. Now, who would want the Jewish religion to be eradicated?

More recently, Muslims have been the target of media propaganda and regularly blamed for terrorist attacks. Wars, too, are common in countries where the Muslim faith is strong, such as Iran, Iraq, Afghanistan, Syria and Nigeria. And there's a reason for this. The Muslim faith prohibits riba (usury) and forbids the charging or paying of interest on all loans, no matter who the loan is with.

The killings really hit home in the United States, however, when the Twin Towers in New York City were destroyed. It might be convenient to blame the disaster on Muslims, but another version of events is far more plausible. Apparently, a group of economic brave-hearts were planning to launch a new independent currency on September 11, 2001, using computers located in the Twin Towers.

# Dire

The global financial elite have been receiving massive amounts of money in interest from both individuals and governments for quite some time. To give you an idea of just how much they receive, the United States government paid $574 billion in interest on its debts in a single year (2019).

Ultra-rich financiers, such as the Rothschilds, already have anything and everything that money can buy, so the extra money they receive in interest payments just sits in a stockpile unused.

By receiving money and not spending it, that money is not returned into the economy, and hence the financiers are effectively extracting money from the global economy on a continual basis. That means the economy shrinks and there is less money available for people to use. That, in turn, places greater pressure on individuals and businesses to obtain money via a loan, wherein new money is created.

In an attempt to prop up the economy during times of economic collapse, governments have borrowed money through the sale of treasury bonds and injected it into the country's economy by spending it on services and infrastructure projects.

But the money that the government borrows must one day be paid back with interest, and so more tax revenue will need to be extracted from people who are already under financial stress.

It's an economic mess on the grandest of scales, and one which has worsened over time.

# Corona

If there's not enough money in the economy, why doesn't the government or central bank just print more of it?

Yes, well. Back in 1862, Abraham Lincoln created the government's own "greenbacks", but he got assassinated for doing so and his beloved greenbacks died with him. From then to the present day, the financial elite have continued to threaten or assassinate any politician who similarly dares to challenge their monopoly of the money supply.

A few political leaders may have the inner fortitude to risk their own life, but no political leader is willing to risk the lives of innocent men and women. The financial elite need merely to threaten to blow up trains, cafes, schools or office buildings to cause politicians to acquiesce.

But all that changed in late 2019 when something remarkable happened – the corona virus.

A new virus wasn't extraordinary because, before then, there had been the SARS virus, the MERS virus, Ebola, bird flu, swine flu, as well as countless others which came and went – not to mention the influenza virus or 'flu which many of us have experienced.

But the corona virus was different.  We were told it was a pandemic that required people to avoid trains, office buildings, restaurants, schools, places of worship, and sports stadiums.

The reason people had to avoid congregating in groups is because, at that time, governments worldwide were printing massive amounts of new money and giving it to the people.  And there was a very real possibility that the financial elite would react negatively.

In late 2019 and 2020, central banks reduced their interest rates to zero and then purchased government bonds using newly-created money.  In essence, the central banks were creating new money and giving it to the government who then gave it to the people.

Previously, central banks dared not create new money because of the threats of global financiers.  But this time, the governments of all countries came together and agreed to print new money simultaneously.  And, what's more, the virus pandemic conveniently provided a valid reason to close borders (preventing the movement of suspected terrorists) and kept innocent people away from public places which terrorists might target.

# Investments

The financial elites are not the only ones who obtain free money by charging interest on the money they loan. Anyone who invests their money is engaging in the same immoral and destructive practice.

An investor might, for example, loan money to a company which is just starting out. Later, when the company is more profitable, it pays the money back to the investor along with an extra amount for interest.

Many individuals give their spare cash or retirement savings to a broker or financial institution which invests their money for them. Here again, any investment returns are funds received which have not been duly earned.

Leasing property is another way of investing one's money. Rather than loaning money directly, the money is used to purchase real estate, and it is the property which is loaned.

Rent, therefore, is a form of interest where a wealthy landlord obtains money despite doing no work and contributing no product or service to society. Those who are unable to purchase their own home must pay rent if they want somewhere to live.

The poor are particularly vulnerable to rent greed. It is a human rights travesty that for every single homeless person in the United States, there are three vacant homes.

Many office buildings are owned by investment trusts and institutions, and the rent they receive contributes to investment returns. So, without even knowing it, your investment portfolio might be making you a partial landlord.

Investments are the means through which money is progressively and continually transferred from the poor to the rich. The poor must borrow money or land in order to live and work, and any interest or rent money they pay makes the wealthy even wealthier.

# Exit

It's easy to identify interest and rent as the cause of all economic problems in the world, but it's quite another thing to undo the mess.

This is because everybody wants to be the landlord or the investor who gets rich by doing nothing. The idea of having a stack of cash, a nest egg, or an investment portfolio which just grows bigger all by itself is enormously appealing to many people.

But for every dollar you receive in interest or rent, it's a dollar that must come from someone else who is poorer than you.

Do you really want to do that?

# Custodian

If you're a landowner, there's a way that you can fairly and reasonably allow others to use your land. Rather than renters, people can be custodians.

A custodian is responsible for the maintenance and care of a property in exchange for the use of it.

When someone is valuing and using an item, it tends to keep its integrity and not fall apart. Nevertheless, wear and tear does occur and that means some items will need to be fixed or replaced. If a custodian is responsible for these costs and work, then they are giving something of great value to the property owner.

Often, too, there are service and utility fees such as rubbish removal, sewerage, electricity, and the maintenance of local roads. These are all costs that can be fairly borne by the land user.

Sometimes accidents occur, such as floods or fires, and a property can be severely damaged. Land users will rarely have the funds to be able to repair and replace expensive items. So, to ensure that the funds are available, the land owner may require the land user to pay insurance.

Property owners can decide who will be a custodian of their land. They can interview potential custodians and do background checks.  In a worst-case scenario, if a custodian is ongoingly not maintaining the property to the land owner's satisfaction, they can be required to leave.

# Shares

When a business needs some extra funds, such as to buy equipment or supplies, it can either borrow money at interest or, alternatively, it can sell shares or stocks.

Shares are not a loan. When a person buys shares in a company, they are buying a part of the company and are becoming a part-owner of the company. Because they are a part-owner, they are able to have some influence on the decisions that the company makes since the company's management are, in effect, the owners' employees.

Shareholders do not receive interest payments, although some stocks – called preferred or priority stocks – do give dividend payouts to the stock-owners four times per year. Dividends are a way of the company sharing its profits with the priority stockholders.

Most shareholders, however, own common stock and do not make their money from receiving dividends. Instead, they watch the share market and aim to buy shares when the shares are cheap and later sell them when they've raised in price. It's an educated gamble with high risks but which can yield high returns.

If you own stock, you are a part-owner of the company. If you own a large proportion of a company's shares or you are a priority shareholder, then you can exert a lot of influence on the decisions that the company's board and management make.

Many businesses, for example, are continually seeking to minimise the wages of employees and increase profitability because that is what the shareholders want.

# Profits

The global financial elites not only loan money to governments and receive interest on those loans, but they also own preferred or priority shares in commercial banks and receive a proportion of the bank's profits via dividends.

The bulk of a commercial bank's profits are derived from interest on loans to customers, and those profits are very large. Even a small bank makes billions of dollars in profit each year and often pays its CEO a million-dollar salary.

Banks are corporations which seek to maximise their profits. And that means getting as much money as they can from customers in interest payments and other fees.

There is a moral dilemma here because banks are the only institution in our society which have the ability to create new money. Wielding the upper hand, banks are able to set the terms and conditions of loan arrangements, and people must either agree to the bank's terms or else go without the money they need.

Banks are also in an incredibly privileged and powerful position because the money held in banks is guaranteed by the government. So, if a bank collapses, it is the government which provides the necessary bailout money whilst the rich shareholders and well-paid management lose nothing.

Fundamentally, banks are civic institutions which should not be privately owned and should not be run so as to maximise profits. They are there to provide an essential service to the community.

Hopefully one day banking corporations will not be able to charge interest on loans.  And, as profitability plummets, private shareholders could sell their shares and stocks to the government, thereby turning banks into public utilities.

# Exchange

In a landmark case back in 1968, an attorney by the name of Jerome Daly challenged the First National Bank of Montgomery in a court case where the bank was seeking to obtain possession of Mr Daly's home so as to pay an outstanding mortgage debt.

Daly won the case, but the decision was later nullified. Nevertheless, the case remains significant because it brought to light a banking practice which had previously been hidden from public view.

When a customer enters into a loan agreement with a bank, they sign a document wherein they promise to pay a certain amount of money in the future. The signed document is therefore a promissory note. The promissory note is held by the bank and listed as an asset on its bookkeeping records.

Some legal minds have argued that the loan contract is not a promissory note because a promissory note is a unilateral obligation to pay and, in contrast, a bilateral contract requires both parties to fulfil certain obligations. But a bank loan contract is not a typical contract between two parties. It involves a statement of offer by the bank, signed by a bank employee, and a separate document signed by the customer who accepts the offer and promises to pay. Also, typical bilateral contracts do not have monetary value in and of themselves, and the fact that the bank holds the loan contract as an asset on its records proves that the customer's promise to pay has monetary value.

After receiving the customer's signed promise to pay, the bank then creates an equivalent amount of credit out of thin air by way of a bookkeeping entry, and gives this credit to the customer who uses it to purchase their home or other item.

In reality, both the customer and the bank are creating new money. But they are creating different types of money.

The customer creates new money in the form of a promissory note. A promissory note has value because it is based upon a living person's promise, which has significant value. On the other hand, the bank's credit is created by merely punching a few numbers into a computer, and so it is not based on anything of real substance. However, the bank's credit is valuable because it can be readily spent to purchase items whereas the customer's promissory note is not liquid or useable money.

The arrangement between the customer and the bank therefore involves an exchange. The customer gives to the bank money which is backed by a promise but which is not spendable, and the bank gives to the customer money which lacks substance but which is spendable. The customer gives to the bank "promisability" whilst the bank gives to the customer "spendability". Overall, there is an exchange of equivalent sums of money but different types of money.

Just because the process is an exchange of one type of money for another type of money, that does not mean that the customer can avoid repaying the principal amount. The customer made a promise to pay, and it was their promise to pay which gave the promissory note its substantial value. It is therefore incumbent upon the customer to abide by their promise and pay the promised amount.

As the customer repays the principal to the bank, the bank removes those amounts from the circulating pool of money in the economy and effectively destroys the credit which it had previously created.

# Loan

This arrangement between a customer and a bank, however, is not a loan.  And it is misleading and deceitful for the bank to call it a loan.

In order for someone to loan an item, they must first be in possession of it and must lose the use of it by loaning it to someone else.  In the case of a bank "loan", the bank gives to the customer money which is newly-created.  It is not money that is otherwise available for the bank to use or give to someone else.

Further, in the arrangement, the bank gives credit to the customer.  Credit is an "I owe you", and it's not possible to loan an "I owe you".

So banks are being quite misleading and even possibly fraudulent (knowingly telling a lie) when they claim that they are loaning money.  But they maintain the falsity because doing so is to their significant financial advantage.

If the arrangement was a bona fide loan where the bank was risking its own money, then it would have a legitimate right to charge the customer interest.  But, because the bank is merely creating and later destroying credit, its demand that a customer pay interest is unjustifiable.

Interest payments on so-called "loans" make up the majority of a commercial bank's profits, so if banks were no longer able to charge interest, then their massive profits would fly out the window.

The bank also has no legitimate right to impose repayment schedules upon customers and charge default fees because the bank is not disadvantaged if a customer decides to repay the principal amount at a later time which is more convenient to them.

If a customer were to die before repaying the principal amount, the bank would be able to take possession of the secured property and sell it to recover the funds to pay any outstanding debt.

Even in a worst-case scenario where the property had dropped in value and insufficient funds were obtained from the sale to repay the outstanding debt, the bank could obtain the money by selling its bad debt to either the central bank or the government.

# Unconscionable

Fraud is unconscionable and renders a contract void and unenforceable, but it would be difficult to prove that the bank knew it was telling a lie when using the word "loan". Instead, the word is misleading or deceiving and needs to be replaced by a more accurate term, such as "credit facility".

Bank "loan" contracts are, however, unconscionable for another reason. They are grossly unfair.

Normally, a contract cannot be criticised for being unfair because it is an agreement that is freely entered into between two parties, and, if one of the parties was stupid enough to agree to a poor bargain, then they have only themselves to blame.

But a bank "loan" contract is different. It's a standard form contract (sometimes called an adhesion contract). A standard form contract is a contract where one party creates it and offers it to another party on a take-it-or-leave-it basis. There is no negotiation of the terms and conditions in a standard form contract.

If you purchase an item from a shop, for example, that arrangement is a standard form contract. The shop offers the item at a certain price, and the customer decides to either purchase it or not. There is no negotiation of the price between the shopkeeper and the customer.

Whilst standard form contracts are efficient and streamline the contract process, they can be abused by powerful organisations.

Banks are in the powerful position of being the only institution in our society which can create new credit, so if an individual or business wants an advance of credit, then their only option is to obtain it from a bank and agree to the bank's terms and conditions. The customer does not have the option of going somewhere else where the contract terms are more fair or favourable because all banks offer essentially the same terms and conditions.

There are laws, at least in Australia, which state that it is unconscionable to create a grossly unfair standard form contract. If the unconscionability is severe and proven to exist, then the party who created the contract can be heavily fined and even jailed.

Whilst it is fair and reasonable for the bank to be paid documentation and administrative fees for the work it performs in creating and destroying the credit and managing the accounts, many of the clauses in a typical bank "loan" contract are grossly unfair and constitute unconscionable conduct. This includes: interest charges; an enforced repayment schedule; default fees; possession of the secured property in the event of default; and the requirement that the customer pay all of the bank's repossession costs and legal fees in the event of a foreclosure.

# Risk

In regard to the payment of interest, a bank might argue that it has a right to charge a customer interest because, even though it is not technically loaning money, it is taking a risk and it should be compensated for that risk. Personally, I don't see how the bank is taking a risk in creating and later removing credit, but, then again, I'm not a banker.

It has been pointed out by a court judge that government regulations require banks to hold a certain amount of money as a type of buffer and that, if customers do not repay the principal when they said they would or do not repay it at all, the bank's buffer is negatively affected.

Since principal repayments are effectively destroyed, I do not see how a buffer of "real" money would be affected. But, in any event, even if the buffer was affected, that does not constitute a risk which customers should pay for in interest charges. Rather, it would be for the government to amend the regulations so as to allow for a more flexible buffer.

The bank has the power, of course, to decide who it does or does not extend credit to, and it can minimise any risk of the credit not being repaid by vetting customers, as well as providing a non-enforceable repayment schedule.

Most significantly, though, as I noted earlier, the bank is not taking a risk because the money held in banks is guaranteed by the government.  So, if a customer dies and sale of the secured property does not recoup sufficient money to pay off the outstanding debt, then the bank could sell its bad debt to the government.

# Tyranny

I've spent many hours pondering what I like to call the "clash of the Titans" – that is, the power struggles between governments and the global financial elite.

And the strange thing is, both consider themselves to be the good guys. The government resents the control and power the financial elite have over the money and economies of the world, and the financial elite resent the laws that governments and monarchies impose upon otherwise free people.

What neither of them realise is that whenever you attempt to control the life of another, you are a tyrant. And this is true regardless of how noble and idealistic your plans and desires are.

Each individual has a right (and a responsibility) to choose for themselves what they consider to be good. That's not to say that all our decisions will be good decisions, but, regardless, we really should have the opportunity to make mistakes and learn from them. When somebody else tells us what to do or makes our decisions for us, we lose that precious learning opportunity. And we lose the satisfaction that comes from making decisions which lead to positive consequences, too.

A wonderful concept called "shared spaces" was developed by a Dutch traffic engineer, Hans Monderman, in the 1980s. His revolutionary idea was to remove all traffic lights, signs, signals and lane markers from roads. Without signals to guide them, motorists, cyclists and pedestrians all had to think for themselves, interact with each other, and negotiate with each other.

The results were extraordinary. Shared spaces have much fewer major accidents, the traffic moves slower, and yet, surprisingly, travel times are reduced. Because it is safer, people are more likely to walk, and the increased foot traffic attracts new shops and apartment buildings to the area.

The message of shared spaces goes beyond road infrastructure, though. It reveals how people thrive and naturally cooperate with each other when given the freedom and responsibility to decide for themselves what they consider appropriate in any given situation.

# Collapse

You might have guessed by now that I'm not a great advocate of governments. And it's true. I am very much looking forward to the day when no one human being has rulership or control over another.

As more people become aware of the all-capitals strawman name and choose to not pay strawman debts such as income taxes, the government will progressively lose its revenue and ability to function.

Some fear that if the government collapsed, all hell would break loose. But the opposite is, in fact, true. Communities thrive, just as they do when traffic signals are removed.

In 2016, Spain had no government because no single political party could win enough seats to form a government. During the time there was no government, the economy boomed, unemployment rates dropped, and people were happier.

In 2013, two economists, John Dawson and John Seater, calculated that if no new regulations had been imposed by the United States government since 1949, the country would now be three times more prosperous than it is.

The rules of governments limit people's freedom to work and trade however they wish. It could even be said that a lot of antisocial behaviour stems from anger and resentment at having been restricted by others who hold positions of authority.

When fewer rules and regulations are imposed, people are more creative, more innovative, more passionate, more productive, more responsible, more caring, and more likely to work cooperatively with each other.

# Decentralisation

The world wide web is a perfect example of a decentralised system. There is no central rulership telling us what we can and cannot do. It is your choice which websites you access. And if you don't like what's available, then you can create your own.

On the internet, all individuals are equals. Whether you're a kid in Kenya or Queen Elizabeth II, each of us is just a bum on a seat staring at a computer screen. There's less discrimination, whether by race, gender, age, or sexuality. We can buy and sell with others anywhere on the globe. We can interact socially with whomever we choose.

But as governments dissolve, public services such as hospitals, schools, pensions and Medicare will need to be replaced with more decentralised systems. Rather than being government funded, such institutions and services will need to be funded by individuals in the community.

And that's a good thing, because it means that only those services that the people actually want will survive and thrive.

Just as we currently give a post, comment or video a thumbs up, there will come a day when we can give an individual, a project, or an organisation a donation of money with the click of a button.

When we interact and work cooperatively in this way – and donate directly to the causes and projects we're passionate about – we become active and eager participants in life.  It's exciting to know that the decisions we make directly help to create the society that we want.

# United States

The United States government has the greatest debt of any country.  Even before the corona virus, it was in debt to the tune of $19 trillion – significantly more than any other country on the planet.  By May 2020, that debt had grown to around $24 trillion.

The government struggles to collect enough tax dollars to pay the interest it owes, let alone pay off any principal.

In the 1980s, President Ronald Regan ordered an investigation into how tax dollars were spent, and the resulting Grace Commission report revealed that all U.S. income tax revenue was used to pay interest on the government's outstanding debts.  Not a single cent went towards paying off the debt itself.  And that was when the government's debt was considerably smaller.

The U.S. government is in a particularly precarious position because its central bank is privately owned.  So, although the Federal Reserve provided the government with trillions of interest-free dollars during the corona virus pandemic, that money is a loan which the government is expected to pay back at some future time via taxes upon the people.  In other countries where the central bank is government-owned, there is no need to pay back the money to the central bank.

Thus, it's abundantly clear that the U.S. government will never be able to repay its debts to either the Federal Reserve or other creditors, and that all taxpayer dollars are going straight down into a bottomless pit.

As less and less people pay these taxes, eventually the government will have to admit the system cannot continue. The corporation that is the United States government will become insolvent and non-functional.

Before that happens, though, the government has a choice to make: does it use its last dying breaths to impose rules upon people, or does it use the remaining resources it has to build bridges into a wonderful new future? A government can, if it so wishes, create web-based interactional systems which enable private individuals to connect and work with each other, ultimately replacing pensions, Medicare, police, and other services with local community-supported hubs.

So, although the United States is in a greater financial pickle than any other country, it has the opportunity to lead the world into a bright new future of freedom, equality, and cooperation.